A Note From Rick Renner

I am on a personal quest to see a "revival of the Bible" so people can establish their lives on a firm foundation that will stand strong and endure the test as end-time storm winds begin to intensify.

In order to experience a revival of the Bible in your personal life, it is important to take time each day to read, receive, and apply its truths to your life. James tells us that if we will continue in the perfect law of liberty — refusing to be forgetful hearers, but determined to be doers — we will be blessed in our ways. As you watch or listen to the programs in this series and work through this corresponding study guide, I trust you will search the Scriptures and allow the Holy Spirit to help you hear something new from God's Word that applies specifically to your life. I encourage you to be a doer of the Word He reveals to you. Whatever the cost, I assure you — it will be worth it.

> Thy words were found, and I did eat them;
> and thy word was unto me the joy and rejoicing of mine heart:
> for I am called by thy name, O Lord God of hosts.
> — Jeremiah 15:16

Your brother and friend in Jesus Christ,

Rick Renner

Rick Renner

The End of Spectator Church
Copyright © 2024 by Rick Renner
1814 W. Tacoma St.
Broken Arrow, OK 74012-1406

Published by Rick Renner Ministries
www.renner.org

ISBN 13: 978-1-6675-0917-4

ISBN 13 eBook: 978-1-6675-0918-1

Rick Renner's guest during this series is Tony Cooke, founder of Tony Cooke Ministries in Tulsa, Oklahoma. Tony is a Bible teacher and author who travels and ministers with his wife, Lisa, strengthening churches and leaders. For more information, go to **tonycooke.org.**

How To Use This Study Guide

This five-lesson study guide corresponds to *"The End of Spectator Church"* *With Rick Renner and Guest Tony Cooke* (Renner TV). Each lesson in this study guide covers a topic that is addressed during the program series, with questions and references supplied to draw you deeper into your own private study of the Scriptures on this subject.

To derive the most benefit from this study guide, consider the following:

First, watch or listen to the program prior to working through the corresponding lesson in this guide. (Programs can also be viewed at **renner.org** by clicking on the Media/Archives links or on our Renner Ministries YouTube channel.)

Second, take the time to look up the scriptures included in each lesson. Prayerfully consider their application to your own life.

Third, use a journal or notebook to make note of your answers to each lesson's Study Questions and Practical Application challenges.

Fourth, invest specific time in prayer and in the Word of God to consult with the Holy Spirit. Write down the scriptures or insights He reveals to you.

Finally, take action! Whatever the Lord tells you to do according to His Word, do it.

For added insights on this subject, it is recommended that you obtain Tony Cooke's book *The End of Spectator Church: Answering God's Call to Full Engagement.*[1] You may also select from Rick's other available resources, such as his book *Fallen Angels, Giants, Monsters, and the World Before the Flood,* by placing your order at **renner.org** or by calling 1-800-742-5593.

TOPIC

What Changed on the Day of Pentecost?

SCRIPTURES

1. **Acts 2:17 (*NLT*)** — "In the last days," God says, "I will pour out my Spirit upon all people. Your sons and daughters will prophesy. Your young men will see visions, and your old men will dream dreams."

SYNOPSIS

The five lessons in this study titled *The End of Spectator Church With Tony Cooke* will focus on the following topics:

- What Changed on the Day of Pentecost?
- Five Ways Believers Function as Priests
- Different Grace — Different Functions
- How Jesus Saw Ministry
- Multi-Dimensional Ministry

In God's Kingdom, each of us is called to be a player in His plans. We are all equipped by His Spirit to carry out a specific function to see souls saved and lives transformed by His power. The time for being a spectator is long gone. It's time for us to get up out of our bleacher-seats and move into action on the field.

The emphasis of this lesson:

Fifty days after Jesus' miraculous resurrection from the dead was the Day of Pentecost — the day that marked the end of "spectator church" From then on, the Holy Spirit of God took up permanent residence inside the hearts of believers, giving everyone from all walks of life the privilege of intimate interaction with God and an opportunity to personally partner with Him in His work.

Many Churches Today Are Simply 'Going Through the Motions'

When the first program opened, Tony Cooke shared a snapshot of his growing years in a mainstream denominational church. As with many churches, the people there had a "spectator" mentality. Week after week, for years on end, people would sit in the pews, singing along from the hymnal and responding occasionally to the readings from God's Word, but that was the extent of their participation.

Although Tony is certainly thankful for the many wonderful things he learned, he acknowledged that his heart was never deeply devoted to God. Sadly, he was going through the motions and never really saw the connection between the hour he spent in church every week and the rest of his life.

Today, we live in a culture where virtually everyone wants to be entertained — including a great many in the Church. But the Church was never meant to be about being entertained. The Church is designed to be a relevant extension of Jesus Christ, dispensing God's Word and empowering people with the Holy Spirit to be Jesus to the world.

While we are to be personal recipients of His Spirit and His Truth, we are also called to be participants in the work of God in the earth. Along with allowing Him to do things *in* us, we must also allow Him to do things *through* us. Even the wonderful teaching and worship that come through media are never just about entertaining us for personal benefit; they are about equipping us for ministry and life.

The truth is, when you go to church and just sit and watch as a spectator, you eventually reach a point of oversaturation where every aspect of the Christian life becomes boring. It's just the same thing week after week, month after month, year after year. This monotony without personal engagement is what leads many people to begin dropping out of church.

The Old Testament Days Were Very Different From New Testament Days

In Old Testament times, man's interaction with God was limited. Through Moses, God gave mankind the Ten Commandments, which were specific instructions on how to interact with God and each other. Indeed, we should all be thankful for the Ten Commandments. As Tony said, "I think the world is better when people respect God and respect others, and I want my neighbor to know and believe that he should not kill me or steal from me."

Nevertheless, the written law of God has a limited effect on people because it works from the *outside* inward to bring about change. When a person receives salvation through Jesus, God's Spirit takes up permanent residence in that person and begins to transform them from the *inside out.* They literally become the righteousness of God in Jesus Christ (*see* 2 Corinthians 5:21).

Exodus 19 talks about how God wanted His people to be *a kingdom of priests.* But when the tangible presence of God showed up, the people were terrified. Filled with fear, they told Moses, "…You speak with us, and we will hear; but let not God speak with us, lest we die" (Exodus 20:19 *NKJV*).

Thus, Moses became the mediator between God and the people. Eventually, Aaron, Moses' brother, became the High Priest. From then on, throughout the entire Old Testament, there was always something between the people and God: Moses and Aaron and the Levitical priestly system, which were all of Aaron's male descendants. The people were dependent on the sacrificial system and the priestly mediation, which God Himself had instituted.

When Jesus rose from the dead, a brand-new scenario was established.

Jesus' death caused the veil in the temple to rip from top to bottom, signifying the opening of the way for people to come directly into God's presence! (*See* Mark 15:38.) Jesus Himself has become our High Priest (*see* Hebrews 4:14-16), and He sits at the right hand of the Father praying and interceding on our behalf (*see* Romans 8:34). The Bible says, "…There is one God, and one mediator between God and men, the man Christ Jesus; who gave himself a ransom for all, to be testified in due time" (1 Timothy 2:5,6).

So while the Old Testament Scriptures and the law were our "schoolmasters" to show us and remind us what sin is, the New Testament teaches us that we are the righteousness of God in Christ. We are now justified (made right with God) by faith and no longer under a schoolmaster (*see* Galatians 3:24-26). Through Jesus, we have a direct connection to God.

The Day of Pentecost Was a Gamechanger

Fifty days after Jesus' miraculous resurrection from the dead was the Day of Pentecost — the day that marked the end of spectator church. On that day, the Holy Spirit of God began taking up permanent residence inside the hearts of believers, making us the very temple in which God lives! (*See* 1 Corinthians 6:19.)

In the days of the Old Testament, the Spirit of God would come upon a person for a specific task, and when that task was done, the Spirit would lift off that person. Prophets, priests, kings, and judges were the primary people whom the Holy Spirit would come upon, and through whom He would work. Everyone else was essentially a spectator, watching from the outside as God moved. Common people never experienced the Spirit of God for themselves.

All that changed on the Day of Pentecost.

Before then, there had never been an entire kingdom where every person became a priest. But that is what the outpouring of the Holy Spirit brought about at Pentecost. First Peter 2:9 declares:

> **But ye are a chosen generation, a royal *priesthood*, an holy nation, a peculiar people; that ye should shew forth the praises of him who hath called you out of darkness into his marvellous light.**

For the first time ever, people from all walks of life were indwelt by the Holy Spirit. The average person who followed God was no longer dependent on the Levitical priests to talk to God on their behalf because Jesus became our High Priest, and we are filled with His very Spirit!

The Outpouring of the Spirit of God Abolished Two Long-Established Barriers

The Scripture says in Acts 2 that when people from around the world saw and heard the Spirit of God speaking and prophesying through uneducated commoners, they were confused and perplexed. Then we read in Acts 2:16-18 that in order to help the people understand what was going on, Peter stood up and said:

> ...This is that which was spoken by the prophet Joel; and it shall come to pass in the last days, saith God, I will pour out of my Spirit upon all flesh: and your sons and your daughters shall prophesy, and your young men shall see visions, and your old men shall dream dreams: and on my servants and on my handmaidens I will pour out in those days of my Spirit; and they shall prophesy.

In this passage, we see two barriers that were broken and removed by the outpouring of the Spirit: the *age barrier* and the *gender barrier*.

For most of us, when we think of a prophet, we picture an old guy with white hair and a beard. This is stereotypical of someone who has access to the Spirit of God and can prophesy. However, God says through the prophet Joel — and repeats through the apostle Peter — that your *sons* and your *daughters* will prophesy. So prophecy is not just for the old folks anymore — it's for the young people too.

Likewise, the gender barrier is broken down. It's not just the men that can house the presence of God and speak on His behalf, but women are also given this same privilege under the New Covenant in Christ. Again, God said, "...Your sons and your *daughters* shall prophesy.... And on my servants and on my *handmaidens* I will pour out in those days of my Spirit; and they shall prophesy." (Acts 2:17,18).

What was once available to a select few is now available to all people. From the day of Pentecost to the present, every believer now has the privilege of receiving the indwelling presence and the empowerment of the person of the Holy Spirit.

When the Holy Spirit was poured out on the people in the upper room, they were *all* filled with the Holy Spirit and began to speak in other tongues (*see* Acts 2:4). The number of people that were in the upper room was 120 (*see* Acts 1:15). So it wasn't just the 11 remaining apostles who were filled with the Spirit that day; it was all 120 people — men *and* women — who were gathered in united prayer and worship.

Among those present on the Day of Pentecost was Mary, the mother of Jesus. Hence, Mary was baptized in the Holy Spirit and prophesied and spoke in other tongues. Clearly, Pentecost was a game-changer because the Spirit was now available for *every* believer. God had removed the barriers of age and gender, enabling every believer to be dynamically empowered by His Spirit.

God Has Called Us To Be a 'Channel' of His Goodness to Others

To be clear, the outpouring of the Holy Spirit was not just for our own benefit. Although we certainly are blessed beyond measure by the indwelling of the Spirit, Jesus said His supernatural power was given to us to be His "witnesses" everywhere we go (*see* Acts 1:8). So the Spirit's empowerment is to benefit us and others through us.

The same is true regarding every revelation of Scripture we receive. When we hear God's Word taught or preached, and the Holy Spirit gives us understanding, it is not just for our own benefit. It is also for the benefit of others. In addition to receiving the truth and being transformed, God wants us to speak the truth to others and become a *transformer*. Freely we have received from Him, and freely we are to give to others (*see* Matthew 10:8).

If all we do is receive good things from God and never give out to others, we will become like the Dead Sea. All it does is receive; it has no outlet into which it pours. Consequently, it is dead.

God intends for us to be a channel through which all His Truth and His power flow.

Some people will look at Rick, who has written dozens of books and has a prolific teaching ministry across the globe, and think, *Well, I can't do what Rick does. I can't write all those books, and I don't have an international television audience like him.* Although most people don't have the extensive reach or the magnitude of impact that Rick has, they can still dive into the Bible and learn from the Holy Spirit what it means for themselves and for others.

The fact is you are not called to be like others — you are called to be the best that "you" you can be. You are to take the truth you learn and share it with those in your sphere of influence. Family members, friends, coworkers, and neighbors all need to see you live and act like Jesus.

If you stop and think about it, on the day of Pentecost, not only did every believer present receive the Holy Spirit, but every believer got off the bench and got into the game. That is exactly what we need to do every day — get off the spiritual bench and get into the game, sharing the message of Jesus with others.

The Empowerment of the Holy Spirit Makes Up for All Our Inadequacies

If you are feeling inferior or inadequate in your ability to be a witness for Jesus, you need to look back at the individuals He called to be His disciples. They were not theologians or people the world would look at and categorize as superior in wisdom. On the contrary, they were fishermen, farmers, and tax collectors who had zero theological training.

Amazingly, God took these individuals who most people would call nobodies, and He changed the world. The truth is, it was *better* that they didn't have any formal, theological training because it greatly reduced the things they needed to unlearn.

Of course, they did have to "get over" themselves and their ungodly, carnal nature. It seems that they were frequently jostling for the top position in Jesus' inner circle, often arguing with each other over who was the best. In their immaturity, they even wanted to call down fire from Heaven and destroy a city that didn't accept Jesus or the Gospel.

When the Holy Spirit came on the Day of Pentecost and began baptizing believers, the rate at which people were transformed into the likeness of Jesus was greatly accelerated. Instead of competing with one another, the disciples really began complementing one another and working together to accomplish Christ's mission. The power of the Spirit filled in the gaps and wiped away inadequacies, which is what He is still doing today.

The Spirit Gives Us Gifts and Develops His Fruit in Our Lives

Once a person is baptized in the Holy Spirit, two powerful things begin to take place. The Spirit gives us unique *gifts* and also goes to work in our lives developing what the Bible calls *fruit* (*see* Galatians 5:22,23). Gifts are given to equip the Church for ministry, and fruit is developed, causing our character to be more and more like Jesus.

Contrary to what you may have been taught, the gifts of the Spirit *and* the fruit of the Spirit are both needed and equally important. Rather than choosing between the two, God wants you to have both. Like the two wings of a plane, the gifts of the Spirit and the fruit of the Spirit work together to bring balance and stability, enabling you to soar and accomplish all that has been assigned to you.

It was the outpouring of the Holy Spirit on the Day of Pentecost that activated all these things in God's people. Since that day, believers from all walks of life have had access to the Spirit's empowerment and the responsibility to *get in the game.* We are not meant to be spectators but participators in God's plans. If you are open and willing to receive the baptism in the Holy Spirit, He will equip you with His gifts and develop His fruit in your life. Empowered by the Spirit, your life will never be the same!

QUESTIONS AND ANSWERS WITH RICK RENNER

In the program, Rick answered the following question from one of our viewers.

Q. What should I do if my pastor is teaching wrong doctrine?

A. If your pastor is teaching wrong doctrine, that is a serious situation. The first thing you should do is to begin to pray for him or her. Pray that he or she is able to clearly hear from God and accurately teach His Word.

Next, pray also for yourself to have ears to hear accurately and clearly what is being taught. It may be that your pastor is teaching right doctrine, and you just don't understand what is being said.

Realize that everyone makes mistakes — including your pastor and you. So pray that God enables your pastor to teach correctly and in alignment with the whole body of God's Word. Pray that you have ears to hear, a mind to understand, and the will to put into practice the truth of His Word.

That being said, if you are attending a church where the pastor is blatantly teaching false doctrine that is contrary to Scripture, then maybe you need to unhitch from that church and move on to another place where you can be sure you're going to be fed a steady diet of God's Word. That will be good for you as well as for your family and friends.

A Prayer To Receive Salvation

If you've never received Jesus as your Savior and Lord, now is the time for you to experience the new life Jesus wants to give you. To receive God's gift of salvation through Jesus, pray this prayer from your heart:

> *Jesus, I repent of my sin and receive You as my Savior and Lord. Wash away my sin with Your precious Blood and make me completely new. I thank You that my sin is removed, and Satan no longer has any right to lay claim on me. Through Your empowering grace, I faithfully promise that I will serve You as my Lord for the rest of my life. In Your name, amen.*

If you just prayed this prayer of salvation, you are born again! You are a brand-new creation in Christ! Would you please let us know of your decision by going to **renner.org/salvation**? We would love to connect with you and pray for you as you begin your new life in Christ.

STUDY QUESTIONS

Study to shew thyself approved unto God, a workman that needeth not to be ashamed, rightly dividing the word of truth.
— 2 Timothy 2:15

1. Tony shared how during his growing up years in church, he was just going through the motions of being a Christian. Think about your own upbringing. Did you grow up in church? If so, were you able to connect what you heard and saw at church with the rest of your life? Or were you just "going through the motions"?

2. When Jesus died, the veil in the Temple was ripped from top to bottom, opening the way for people to come directly into God's presence! This fact appears in Matthew 27:50 and 51; Mark 15:37 and 38; and Luke 23:44-46. Carefully read these passages along with Hebrews 4:14-16 and Ephesians 3:12 and describe what the Holy Spirit shows you about what Jesus' death and resurrection restored to you.

PRACTICAL APPLICATION

But be ye doers of the word, and not hearers only, deceiving your own selves.
—James 1:22

1. Among those present on the Day of Pentecost was Mary, the mother of Jesus. Hence, Mary was baptized in the Holy Spirit, enabling her to prophesy and speak in other tongues. How does this fact change your perspective of Mary and of the importance of the Spirit's baptism?
2. According to Galatians 5:22 and 23, what are the fruits of the Spirit? Which of these can you see most clearly in your life today that you couldn't see two or three years ago? Which one(s) would you like to see operating more in your life?
3. Are you personally benefiting from the Holy Spirit's empowerment? If so, how? And how is the Spirit's empowerment benefiting others in your life?

LESSON 2

TOPIC

Five Ways Believers Function as Priests

SCRIPTURES

1. **Acts 2:5,9 (*NKJV*)** — And there were dwelling in Jerusalem Jews, devout men, from every nation under heaven. Parthians and Medes and Elamites, those dwelling in Mesopotamia, Judea and Cappadocia, Pontus and Asia.
2. **Romans 12:1,2 (*NKJV*)** — I beseech you therefore, brethren, by the mercies of God, that you present your bodies a living sacrifice, holy, acceptable to God, *which is* your reasonable service. And do not be conformed to this world, but be transformed by the renewing of your mind, that you may prove what is that good and acceptable and perfect will of God.

SYNOPSIS

Everything changed on the Day of Pentecost. That's the moment when believers from all walks of life were first empowered by the Person of the Holy Spirit. God spoke through the prophet Joel, and then again through the apostle Peter, saying, "And it shall come to pass in the last days, saith God, I will pour out of my Spirit upon all flesh: and your sons and your daughters shall prophesy, and your young men shall see visions, and your old men shall dream dreams: and on my servants and on my handmaidens I will pour out in those days of my Spirit; and they shall prophesy" (Acts 2:17,18).

For the first time, it wasn't just the prophet, the priest, the judge, or the king who flowed in the power of the Holy Spirit as it had been in Old Testament times. It was now young men and women — including manservants and maidservants — who were prophesying. The Day of Pentecost marked the beginning of a new era in which the barriers of age and gender were broken. Young and old, male and female, from all walks of life were now given the privilege of speaking on God's behalf. Likewise, all believers began to function as priests in His Kingdom.

The emphasis of this lesson:

The five ways we as believers function as priests include: (1) offering ourselves, including our bodies, to God; (2) worshiping, praising, and praying; (3) serving others; (4) giving; and (5) evangelizing or sharing the Gospel.

Through Christ, We Are a Holy, Royal Priesthood

Friend, if you have repented of your sin and invited Jesus to be your Lord and Savior, you have been washed in His precious Blood, and His Spirit is living in you. That makes you a member of God's "holy priesthood" and part of a "nation of priests." We find this truth described in Peter's first letter, where he declares:

> **You also, as living stones, are being built up a spiritual house, *a holy priesthood*, to offer up spiritual sacrifices acceptable to God through Jesus Christ.**
>
> **— 1 Peter 2:5 (*NKJV*)**

When Peter wrote this passage, he was talking to Christians all throughout Asia Minor, the area we know today as modern Turkey. At the time of this writing, the Temple in Jerusalem was about to be destroyed — or had already been destroyed — by the Romans. Accordingly, God was building a new temple where each believer was (and is) a living stone that He is strategically joining together to form a new spiritual house in which to live.

The Church — also known as the Body of Christ — is this new spiritual house, and each believer is a priest who serves within it. Unlike the priests of the Old Testament who offered lambs, goats, and doves as sacrifices, we offer *spiritual* sacrifices that are acceptable to God through Jesus Christ.

This idea of believers being priests is repeated in First Peter 2:9 where Peter says:

> **But you are a chosen generation, a royal priesthood, a holy nation, His own special people, that you may proclaim the praises of Him who called you out of darkness into His marvelous light.**

Here, through Peter, the Holy Spirit tells us we are *a royal priesthood*, and the fact that we are priests of God's new covenant through Christ means we are not spectators. Instead, we are active participants engaged in the work of the Lord.

Priesthood Gives Us the Privilege of Access to God

Although many mistakenly believe that pastors are the ones called by God to do just about everything in ministry, that is not the case. Yes, pastors are very important in God's overall plan. They are one of the fivefold ministry gifts given to the Church to equip believers for the work of the ministry (*see* Ephesians 4:11,12). However, because we are *all* priests in God's Kingdom, we share in the Lord's work and have the same level of access to God that pastors have.

The privilege of priesthood is that every believer has equal access to God through Jesus Christ. When you go to God in prayer, you don't have to say, "Heavenly Father, I come to You right now in the name of Jesus and Rick Renner or Tony Cooke." It's *through Jesus alone* we have access to the throne of God's grace (*see* Hebrew 4:15,16). Scripture says:

There is salvation in no one else! God has given no other name under heaven by which we must be saved.

— Acts 4:12 (*NLT*)

...There is one God and one Mediator between God and men, the Man Christ Jesus.

— 1 Timothy 2:5 (*NKJV*)

The reason we as priests have access to God is because of our High Priest Jesus. To be clear, the idea of priesthood has nothing to do with the structure or hierarchal positions of different denominations that use this term. The New Testament clearly reveals that *every* believer serves as a priest in God's Kingdom.

Again, this is not to minimize the job or calling of pastors. They are anointed by God to teach, equip, encourage, comfort, and lead believers in the right direction. But pastors are not called to be mediators between God and the people they lead. Rather, they are called to teach people how to have faith in Jesus and come to God through Him.

Your pastor is gifted to teach you what the Bible says and help you tap into the truth of who you are in Christ. The more revelation you receive of what Jesus has done for you, the more confidence you will have to fearlessly and boldly approach God's throne to receive His mercy for your failures and His grace (ability and strength) in your time of need to do whatever He is asking.

As Priests, We Help Others in Their Relationship With the Father

If you study the Old Testament and learn what priests did under the old covenant, you will better understand what we as priests are called to do under the new covenant. For example, priests used to help people come to the temple and bring their sacrifices to God. Likewise, priests would pray to God on behalf of the people, interceding for their needs.

In a similar way, as priests of the New Covenant in Christ, a big part of our ministry is to help people come to the altar of God and bring an appropriate, acceptable sacrifice to Him, which includes the sacrifice of our lives. We are also to serve as prayer partners, lifting up the needs of others to the Father on their behalf. If you're born again, you are a priest who has been activated to serve and help other worshipers.

Now, being a priest does not elevate us or make us spiritually independent. On the contrary, we are part of a holy, royal *priesthood*. The Bible doesn't say, "You are a royal priest." It says, "You are a…royal *priesthood*" (1 Peter 2:9). So just as the Old Testament priests worked together under the supervision of their high priest, we too are to work together under the supervision of Jesus, our High Priest.

There is nothing wrong with having a hierarchy of leaders. That structure helps the entire priesthood function collectively as a team to serve God's people. Priests who broke rank and went rogue, attempting to do their own thing, came under God's judgment. Aaron's sons and Eli's sons are perfect examples (*see* Leviticus 10:1-3; 1 Samuel 2:12-25). We must do things God's way in order to experience His blessings.

Five Ways We as Believers Function as Priests

#1: We function as priests when we *offer ourselves, including our bodies, to God*.

Romans 12:1 and 2 (*NKJV*) says, "I beseech you therefore, brethren, by the mercies of God, that you present your bodies a living sacrifice, holy, acceptable to God, which is your reasonable service. And do not be conformed to this world, but be transformed by the renewing of your mind, that you may prove what is that good and acceptable and perfect will of God."

If you think about it, Old Testament priests had it easier because they only had to bring an animal to God and sacrifice it on the altar. As New Testament priests, we have to offer our own bodies to God as a living sacrifice. In other words, we are the first thing we need to sacrifice to God. Thus, priesthood means we are consecrated to God. It is a dedication and total surrender of ourselves to Him.

Rick said, "I start every day of my life by reading my Bible and surrendering myself to God. I say, 'Lord, I give you my mind, I give you my body, I give you my spirit, I give you everything that I am.' I pray that every single morning because I believe the first thing that I am to do as a member of the royal priesthood is to bring *myself* to the altar of God."

Keep in mind that while priesthood provides us privileges, it also involves responsibility. And if we don't understand and operate in both aspects, we won't be functioning in our priesthood as much as we should.

#2: We function as priests when we *worship*, *praise*, and *pray*.

One of the things that the priests in the Old Testament did was *minister unto the Lord*. Many times, we want God to minister to us, which is a wonderful part of our relationship with Him. But ministry should be a two-way street.

Again and again, the Bible tells us that the Levite priests ministered to the Lord. Likewise, it says Aaron and Moses as well as Samuel and David ministered to the Lord (*see* 1 Chronicles 23:13; 1 Samuel 3:1; Jeremiah 33:22). In the same way, our life is to minister to the Lord. When we sing, we're not just singing a song; we're ministering to the Lord, and we can do that anywhere we are.

#3: We function as priests when we *serve*.

Old Testament priests lived their entire lives serving in the temple, performing many different tasks. What is interesting is that when Mary, Lazarus' sister, took the jar of costly perfume and poured it on Jesus' feet and then wiped His feet with her hair (*see* John 12:3), it was an act of service symbolic to that of the temple priests. Instead of using water and a towel to wash and dry Jesus' feet, which was a customary expression of hospitality, Mary used precious oil and her hair. This profound act had priestly elements.

The Bible says, "…And the house was filled with the fragrance of the perfume" (John 12:3 *NIV*). This verse is filled with priestly language and depicts the service of a priest. When a believer, or a group of believers, follows Mary's example and serves the Lord in this way, it is a powerful demonstration of New Testament priesthood. Remember, Jesus said, "…Assuredly, I say to you, inasmuch as you did it to one of the least of these My brethren, you did it to Me" (Matthew 25:40 *NKJV*).

Even though you can't directly minister to Jesus, when you go out of your way and use your resources to minister to others, Jesus said you have done it to Him.

#4: We function as priests when we *give*.

When Paul received an offering from the Philippian believers, he described it as "…a sweet-smelling aroma, an acceptable sacrifice, well pleasing to God" (Philippians 4:18 *NKJV*). Once more, we see the actions of believers described as a sweet-smelling fragrance unto God. This, too, is priestly language depicting priestly functions.

In the Old Testament, when someone said, "Let's go to the temple and worship," they were not saying, "Let's go hear a sermon," or, "Let's go sing a few songs." What they were really saying was, "Let's go and give God something! Let's go and make a sacrifice to Him."

This tells us that giving should not just be mechanically going through the motions. It should be us offering something of value to God from our heart.

#5: We function as priests when we *evangelize*.

When we share the good news of Jesus Christ with others, we are operating in the office of New Testament priests.

Paul talked about this in his letter to the Romans. He said God had given him grace, that he "…might be a minister of Jesus Christ to the Gentiles, ministering the gospel of God, that the offering of the Gentiles might be acceptable, sanctified by the Holy Spirit" (Romans 15:16 *NKJV*).

In the Old Testament, one requirement of the priesthood was that they be trained to answer people's questions. In the same way, we as believers have the responsibility to respectfully answer people's questions and share the Gospel with them.

That is why after Peter wrote about us being a holy, royal priesthood, he also wrote in the same letter and said, "…Always be prepared to give an answer to everyone who asks you to give the reason for the hope that you have. But do this with gentleness and respect" (1 Peter 3:15 *NIV*).

These are the five ways we as believers function as New Testament priests. In our next lesson, we will examine how the Holy Spirit gives us different aspects of grace to carry out specific functions.

QUESTIONS AND ANSWERS WITH RICK RENNER

In the program, Rick answered the following question from one of our viewers.

Q. How do I enforce daily Bible-reading in my life?

A. I made a personal rule in my life that I live by, and that rule is *no Bible, no breakfast.*

Now, that is not a biblical rule, but it's a rule that I need in my life. Every day, I know that if I don't read my Bible, I will not be eating breakfast — and maybe not eating anything that entire day.

If I want to eat physical food, I have to first put spiritual food into my heart. Why would I feed my physical body to keep it strong, but forget that my spirit needs to be strong too? When you feed yourself the Word of God, you literally strengthen your inner man.

Friend, begin to make a daily decision to feed your spirit the Word of God. The rule of *no Bible, no breakfast* is strong, but if you adopt it for yourself, you will begin to experience spiritual health and growth on a scale like you have never seen before!

A Prayer To Receive Salvation

If you've never received Jesus as your Savior and Lord, now is the time for you to experience the new life Jesus wants to give you. To receive God's gift of salvation through Jesus, pray this prayer from your heart:

> *Jesus, I repent of my sin and receive You as my Savior and Lord. Wash away my sin with Your precious Blood and make me completely new. I thank You that my sin is removed, and Satan no longer has any right to lay claim on me. Through Your empowering grace, I faithfully promise that I will serve You as my Lord for the rest of my life. In Your name, amen.*

If you just prayed this prayer of salvation, you are born again! You are a brand-new creation in Christ! Would you please let us know of your decision by going to **renner.org/salvation**? We would love to connect with you and pray for you as you begin your new life in Christ.

STUDY QUESTIONS

Study to shew thyself approved unto God, a workman that needeth not to be ashamed, rightly dividing the word of truth.
— 2 Timothy 2:15

1. The privilege of priesthood is that every believer has equal access to God through Jesus Christ. Take a few moments to reflect on these key verses and jot down what the Holy Spirit reveals to you about entering God's presence and interacting with Him.

- Who gives you access to a relationship with the Father?
  (*See* John 10:9; 14:6; Romans 5:1,2; Ephesians 2:18.)

- What gives you the right to enter God's presence?
  (*See* Hebrews 10:19-22.)

- How does God want you to approach Him?
  (*See* Ephesians 3:12; Hebrews 4:15,16.)

2. Of the five ways we as believers function as priests, which one were you aware of, and which one is new to you? Which of these functions are operating in your life, and in what ways are they visible?

PRACTICAL APPLICATION

> But be ye doers of the word, and not hearers only,
> deceiving your own selves.
> — James 1:22

1. As a believer, you are God's priest, and as His priest, you are called to help others in their relationship with the Father. Who has God used in your life to help you connect deeper in your relationship with Him? Who has prayed for and with you and showed you how to live in a way that pleases God? Who are you influencing in these same ways?

2. Take a few moments to read and reflect on the powerful instruction of Romans 12:1 and 2 (*NLT*):

   And so, dear brothers and sisters, I plead with you to give your bodies to God because of all he has done for you. Let them be a living and holy sacrifice — the kind he will find acceptable. This is truly the way to worship him. Don't copy the behavior and customs of this world, but let God transform you into a new person by changing the way you think. Then you will learn to know God's will for you, which is good and pleasing and perfect.

   Are you walking in obedience to this command? Being honest with yourself, consider the areas in which you need God's grace to surrender yourself more fully. What are some practical steps you can take to come up higher and be a "living sacrifice"?

TOPIC

Different Grace — Different Functions

SCRIPTURES

1. **1 Peter 4:10,11** — As every man hath received the gift, even so minister the same one to another, as good stewards of the manifold grace of God. If any man speak, let him speak as the oracles of God; if any man minister, let him do it as of the ability which God giveth: that God in all things may be glorified through Jesus Christ, to whom be praise and dominion for ever and ever. Amen.

2. **1 Peter 4:10,11 (*NLT*)** — God has given each of you a gift from his great variety of spiritual gifts. Use them well to serve one another. Do you have the gift of speaking? Then speak as though God himself were speaking through you. Do you have the gift of helping others? Do it with all the strength and energy that God supplies. Then everything you do will bring glory to God through Jesus Christ. All glory and power to him forever and ever! Amen.

3. **Romans 12:6-8** — Having then gifts differing according to the grace that is given to us, whether prophecy, let us prophesy according to the proportion of faith; or ministry, let us wait on our ministering: or he that teacheth, on teaching; or he that exhorteth, on exhortation: he that giveth, let him do it with simplicity; he that ruleth, with diligence; he that sheweth mercy, with cheerfulness.

4. **Romans 12:6-8 (*NLT*)** — In his grace, God has given us different gifts for doing certain things well. So if God has given you the ability to prophesy, speak out with as much faith as God has given you. If your gift is serving others, serve them well. If you are a teacher, teach well. If your gift is to encourage others, be encouraging. If it is giving, give generously. If God has given you leadership ability, take the responsibility seriously. And if you have a gift for showing kindness to others, do it gladly.

SYNOPSIS

In Lesson 1, we saw how the outpouring of the Holy Spirit on the Day of Pentecost changed everything. On that day, all 120 believers who were obediently waiting in the Upper Room for the promise of the Father, were baptized in the Holy Spirit and began to boldly function in various gifts of God's grace.

In Lesson 2, we noted that as believers, we are part of a holy, royal *priesthood* (*see* 1 Peter 2:5,9), and God has called us to function as His priests of the New Covenant under the supervision of our High Priest, Jesus Christ. Five specific ways we function as priests are offering ourselves, including our bodies, to God; worshiping, praising, and praying; serving others; giving; and evangelizing or sharing the Gospel.

The emphasis of this lesson:

Through the finished work of Jesus, God has poured out His grace into the lives of every single believer and given us special spiritual gifts. The variety of these gifts is great, and not everyone has the same gift. Once we know what our gift is, we must fully embrace it and develop it over time in order to maximize its effectiveness.

God Wants Us To Pour Into the Lives of Others

Through the indwelling presence of the Holy Spirit, we are no longer spectators, but active participants in the Kingdom of God, bringing about His purpose and plan in the lives of people all over the world.

Instead of being like the Dead Sea, which has no life in it because it has no outlet, we are to pour God's goodness into the lives of others. Scientists say that if they could create an outlet for the Dead Sea, its waters would come alive. But it remains dead because all it does is receive.

As a Christian, when you only receive and never give out, you become stagnant, and in that position, you'll never thrive. You must have an outlet of others into whom you can pour. That outlet can be coworkers, people at church, or individuals in the community. You need somewhere and someone you can serve — you need people with whom you can share the revelation of truth you've received.

Jesus said, "…Freely you have received, freely give" (Matthew 10:8 *NKJV*). The more you let God's goodness flow through you, the more He will get to you. Becoming an active participant in God's plan causes the life of His Spirit to flourish in your own life. Proverbs 11:25 (*MSG*) confirms this, declaring, "The one who blesses others is abundantly blessed; those who help others are helped."

Everyone, Without Exception, Has Received a Gift From God

In Peter's first epistle, he wrote to multiple congregations of believers over a wide geographical area. Under the anointing of the Holy Spirit, Peter said:

> **God has given each of you a gift from his great variety of spiritual gifts. Use them well to serve one another.**
> **— 1 Peter 4:10 (*NLT*)**

Interestingly, Rick has made this verse a personal declaration of faith for his life. Every time he stands to minister, he says, "Lord, You said You have given every man a spiritual gift, and You've specifically graced me to teach. Therefore, I'm embracing that gift. I ask You, Lord, to use me mightily. In Jesus' name."

Although not everyone has the gift of teaching like Rick, the Bible does say, "*Every man* hath received the gift…" (1 Peter 4:10). In Greek, the word "every" is *hekastos*, and it means *every single person without exception*. This tells us that if you are a child of God, you have received at least one specific spiritual gift from Him. The word "gift" here is the Greek word *charisma*, which describes a *grace-given gift*. When you receive a grace-given gift, you are empowered to do what you could never do by yourself.

Apart from God's anointing, Rick would never naturally be able to speak into the lens of a camera. But because the grace of God has empowered him to teach, he is able to stand week after week, year after year, and do what he would never be able to do on his own. In the same way, there is a special grace from God operating in *your* life that will empower you to do what you could never do on your own. It is supernatural, and when you choose to take hold of it on purpose, it will grow.

Looking again at First Peter 4:10, it says, "Every man hath received the gift…." The word "received" in Greek is a form of the word *lambano*, which means *to receive*, but it also means *to take*. The use of this word tells us that although God gives us these marvelous gifts, we must choose to *take* them and make them our own. Thus, the word *lambano* implies *ownership* and *management* of what God gives us.

Friend, you must receive the gift God has given you, and then make a decision to wrap your arms around it and make it your own. This includes developing your gift and learning how to manage it. Once you know the special gift of grace God has given you, you must take it by faith and say, "Thank You, Lord, for this gift! I choose to wrap my arms around it, develop it, and use it to be a blessing to others."

Our Gifts Must Be Developed Over Time

Now, just because a person has a gift from God doesn't mean it is fully developed the moment it's received. It takes time and effort to learn how to work with the Holy Spirit and cultivate our gift so that it reaches maximum impact in and through our life.

Think about Usain Bolt, the Jamaican sprinter who is considered to be the greatest sprinter of all time. As gifted as he is, he did not emerge from his mother's womb able to run at top speed. On the contrary, he had to first learn how to crawl, then walk, and finally how to run. His Olympic-level running game didn't just suddenly appear. It took Usain years of rigorous training and conditioning to become the gold medalist we know today.

The same principle holds true for every gift God gives. Whether it's writing, cooking, teaching, building, giving, or administrating, the gifts God gives us must be fully embraced and developed over time in order to maximize their effectiveness. We must practice, practice, and practice some more. It is practice that perfects one's gift. Indeed, repetition is the mother of excellence.

By giving yourself to your gift again and again and again, you develop it in extraordinary ways.

Guard Against Comparing Yourself With Others

Again, First Peter 4:10 (*NLT*) says, "God has given each of you a gift from his great *variety* of spiritual gifts. Use them well to serve one another." The fact that God has a great variety of gifts means not all of us are going to have the same gift, which is a blessing. If everyone had the very same gift, life would be boring, and everyone would be lacking and deficient in many areas.

Just as it takes a variety of vitamins, macronutrients, and micronutrients to produce a healthy, well-balanced body physically, it takes a variety of spiritual gifts to produce a healthy, well-balanced spiritual *Body of Christ*. Not one gift is better than another — all gifts are equally important and needed by all believers.

One of the worst things we can do is *compare* ourselves with other believers. As Teddy Roosevelt is noted as saying, "Comparison is the thief of joy." Indeed, it is a deadly trap of the enemy that will rob us and the world of our gift if we let it. In Second Corinthians 10:12, the apostle Paul wrote that those who compare themselves among themselves are *not* wise.

Rick shared how he fell prey to this tendency in the early days of his ministry. He would look at seasoned ministers and begin to think, *I don't preach and teach like them. They have such a powerful way of delivering the Word that I just can't duplicate.* Rick had to come to the place where he was comfortable in his own gifting. It took time, but eventually, a moment finally came when he stopped trying to be like everyone else, and he learned to embrace the unique gift of grace in his own life.

The fact is that everyone sparkles a little differently, and that puts each of us in a unique niche of our own. If everyone had the same gifts, some of us would not be needed.

Not Everyone Has the Same Gifts

After telling us that God has given each of us a gift from the great variety of spiritual gifts, Peter went on to say:

> **Do you have the gift of speaking? Then speak as though God himself were speaking through you. Do you have the gift of helping others? Do it with all the strength and energy that God supplies. Then everything you do will bring glory to God through Jesus Christ. All glory and power to him forever and ever! Amen.**
>
> **— 1 Peter 4:11 (*NLT*)**

Notice Peter didn't say, "Since you all have the gift of speaking," or "Since you all have the gift of helping others." Instead, he asks the questions: "Do you have the gift of speaking?" and "Do you have the gift of helping others?" The fact that he asks these questions tells us not everyone has the same gifts.

Tabitha (also known as Dorcas) is a perfect example. We have no record in Scripture of her ever preaching or teaching a single sermon. Yet her *life* was preaching and teaching nonstop. Clearly, she was gifted by God to make things with her hands. Using a needle, thread, and fabric, she became well-known for making various types of clothing. In fact, she was so admired for her gift that when she became ill and died, the community sought out Peter to come and pray for her to be raised from the dead, which is exactly what happened (*see* Acts 9:36-41).

God wants you to use the gift He has uniquely placed in you!

Peter said, "Do you have the gift of speaking? Then speak as though God himself were speaking through you. Do you have the gift of helping others? Do it with all the strength and energy that God supplies" (1 Peter 4:11 *NLT*). This instruction applies to any gift God has given you. When you use your gift with all the strength and energy God supplies, "…Then everything you do will bring glory to God through Jesus Christ…" (1 Peter 4:11 *NLT*).

Interestingly, Peter's statement that we are to use our gifts *with all the strength and energy that God supplies* means that God is in partnership with us. Not only does He give us the gift, but He also supplies the strength and energy to use it. God will help us! And His power will flow through us! Our job is to embrace the gift and make the daily decision to develop it and operate in it. God's power will kick in and take our gift where it needs to go.

Everyone's Gift Is Important!

Again, there are a variety of gifts that God gives. Some people have a gift to cook and bake delicious meals that they can take to people in need. Others are gifted by God with mathematical abilities and the understanding of technology. Still others are skilled at things like offering wise counsel, managing people, and caring for children.

Some may say, "Those gifts are not very spiritual," but that isn't true! Anyone who is filling a need and producing good results is a gift to others. Take caring for children for example. Jesus said, "And if anyone gives even a cup of cold water to one of these little ones who is my disciple, truly I tell you, that person will certainly not lose their reward" (Matthew 10:42 *NIV*).

Consider Rick's TV show. Without question, Rick is gifted to teach the Word of God with great precision and power. But what would happen if he had no one who was gifted to build the TV set, operate a camera, run the audio, and or edit the program? All these tasks require people who are gifted — not to mention the multitude of ministry partners who pray for and pay for the programs to be produced and aired across the globe.

Every single gift is important — regardless of what it is.

If someone in the Body of Christ is not functioning in their God-given gift, everyone else is affected. Just as the physical body is made of many parts, the Body of Christ is just as diverse. Some function as hands, feet, arms, and legs, while others function as the eyes, ears, nose, and mouth. Many in the Body are seemingly invisible, functioning undercover like one's pancreas, liver, or kidneys. But what would the body be without the kidneys or the liver? Could one function without lungs or blood vessels? *Of course not!*

Every single part is important. Thus, every person's gift is equally valuable.

Encouraging, Giving, and Leading Are Also God-Given Gifts

It is interesting to note that the apostle Paul seemed to echo Peter's words in Romans 12. Speaking of gifts, he wrote:

> **In his grace, God has given us different gifts for doing certain things well. So if God has given you the ability to prophesy, speak out with as much faith as God has given you. If your gift is serving others, serve them well. If you are a teacher, teach well. If your gift is to encourage others, be encouraging. If it is giving, give generously. If God has given you leadership ability, take the responsibility seriously. And if you have a gift for showing kindness to others, do it gladly.**
> **— Romans 12:6-8 (*NLT*)**

Here, again, we read about the gifts of prophecy and teaching, but Paul also mentions the gift of encouraging others as well as giving generously. These are actual grace-gifts from God that are essential to the health of the Church.

Take the gift of giving. There are some people who are graced by God to make money and give generously to fund ministries and provide for individuals in need. In fact, for these folks, offering time at church is their favorite part of the service. You may know someone with this gift, or you may be a God-called giver yourself. If you are, *give generously*! And don't let the enemy make you feel guilty or that your gift is less valuable than someone else's gift to teach or preach.

As strange as it may sound, some God-called givers are working to get to the point where they live on 10 percent of their income and give away 90 percent to advance God's Kingdom. The gift of giving is needed — just as much as the gift of prophecy, the gift of teaching, the gift of encouraging, and every other gift God has given.

Leadership and showing mercy and kindness to others are two more powerful grace gifts. Paul said, "…If God has given you leadership ability, take the responsibility seriously. And if you have a gift for showing kindness to others, do it gladly" (Romans 12:8 *NLT*). Whatever God has gifted you to do, He wants you to do it with all your might! (*See* Ecclesiastes 9:10.)

Excitement and Fulfillment Are Found When You're Functioning in Your Gifts

In all these God-given gifts, there is a *give* and a *take*. God *gives* us the gift, but we must purposely choose to *take* the gift and operate in it. The more we flow and function in our gift, the more it is developed and the more impact it will have.

No one should operate in their gifts because someone makes them feel guilty or pressured. All of us should be motivated internally by the Spirit of God to function in the gifts He gives. Second Corinthians 9:7 (*NKJV*) communicates this clearly, telling us, "So let each one give *as he purposes in his heart*, not grudgingly or of necessity; for God loves a cheerful giver." Our response should be to the stirring of the Holy Spirit in our hearts — not the external pressure or the emotional hype of others.

You will find that the greatest sense of fulfillment and excitement in your life will come as you are operating in your God-given gift.

If you are bored with life and lacking in joy, you should probably stop and prayerfully evaluate what you are doing. When you are doing what God has called and equipped you to do, you will experience a sense of pleasure and satisfaction that cannot be experienced in any other way.

This applies equally to those who are called to teach, preach, lead, encourage, show mercy, give, and help others. All the various aspects of ministry require people who are gifted to be visibly out in front as well as those who are gifted to be behind the scenes. As one evangelist from the 1800s once said, "For every one revival leader, we need one hundred helpers."

Friend, don't believe the lie that you are not needed. God has uniquely gifted you to do what others can't. It's time to stand up and step out of the bleachers and take your place on God's playing field. Time is short and the stakes are high. Give yourself to your gift so that souls can be saved, and lives can be changed for eternity.

QUESTIONS AND ANSWERS WITH RICK RENNER

In the program, Rick answered the following question from one of our viewers.

Q. How do I grow spiritually?

A. In First Timothy 4:7, the Bible says, "But refuse profane and old wives' fables, and exercise thyself rather unto godliness." This verse tells us that there are certain spiritual disciplines or exercises that we need to be doing in our life if we want to grow spiritually.

Some of the proven, basic practices that produce spiritual growth include reading the Bible regularly, spending time in God's presence, praying, obeying the promptings of the Holy Spirit, and being a part of a healthy local church. When you begin to do these essentials, you begin to use your muscles and exercise spiritually. This produces healthy spiritual growth and development. Regardless of who you are, if you practice these basic components of spiritual exercise, you will grow spiritually.

For more about spiritual growth, we encourage you to get Rick's series entitled *How To Develop Spiritually*. You can order it at **renner.org** or by calling 1-800-742-5593.

A Prayer To Receive Salvation

If you've never received Jesus as your Savior and Lord, now is the time for you to experience the new life Jesus wants to give you. To receive God's gift of salvation through Jesus, pray this prayer from your heart:

> *Jesus, I repent of my sin and receive You as my Savior and Lord. Wash away my sin with Your precious Blood and make me completely new. I thank You that my sin is removed, and Satan no longer has any right to lay claim on me. Through Your empowering grace, I faithfully promise that I will serve You as my Lord for the rest of my life. In Your name, Amen.*

If you just prayed this prayer of salvation, you are born again! You are a brand-new creation in Christ! Would you please let us know of your decision by going to **renner.org/salvation**? We would love to connect with you and pray for you as you begin your new life in Christ.

STUDY QUESTIONS

> **Study to shew thyself approved unto God, a workman that needeth not to be ashamed, rightly dividing the word of truth.**
> **— 2 Timothy 2:15**

1. The New Testament has much to say about spiritual gifts. Take time to read these three key passages and identify the specific gifts that are mentioned in each. How are these passages similar? How are they different? What new insights is the Holy Spirit showing you about the gifts He has given to God's people?

   • Romans 12:4-8

   • 1 Corinthians 12:4-11

   • 1 Corinthians 12:27-31

   • Ephesians 4:11-16

2. To help us avoid the deceptive and dangerous trap of *comparison*, the Holy Spirit prompted Paul to write the very important words found in First Corinthians 12:12-27. Carefully read through this passage (in two or three different Bible versions). What would life be like if everyone had the same gift or function? How does the imagery of the physical body help you better understand and appreciate the gifts in

others? What else is God revealing to you about the gifts in your life and the lives of others?

PRACTICAL APPLICATION

But be ye doers of the word, and not hearers only,
deceiving your own selves.
— James 1:22

1. First Peter 4:10 tells us that God has given each and every person — *without exception*—a special gift. Do you know what gift (or gifts) God has given *you*? If so, what is it? Are you operating in and developing your gift(s)?

2. What gifts in others has God used to bless and strengthen you and your family? Describe one crucial situation or pivotal moment when someone operated in their God-given gift, and it was a game-changer in your life.

3. Are you comfortable in your own gifting? Take some time to pray and say, "Lord, please forgive me for comparing and competing with others. Deliver me from feelings of inferiority and the fear of having no purpose. Give me the grace to embrace the gift(s) You have placed in me and help me value and appreciate the gifts in others that I don't have. I love You, Lord, and I welcome Your presence in my life to help fully develop my gifts. Anoint and bless all that I do in obedience to You that You may receive glory. In Jesus' name, amen!"

LESSON 4

TOPIC

How Jesus Saw Ministry

SCRIPTURES

1. **Matthew 9:35-37** — And Jesus went about all the cities and villages, teaching in their synagogues, and preaching the gospel of the kingdom, and healing every sickness and every disease among the people. But when he saw the multitudes, he was moved with compassion on them, because they fainted, and were scattered abroad, as sheep having

no shepherd. Then saith he unto his disciples, The harvest truly is plenteous, but the labourers are few.

2. **Matthew 9:35-38 (*NLT*)** — Jesus traveled through all the towns and villages of that area, teaching in the synagogues and announcing the Good News about the Kingdom. And he healed every kind of disease and illness. When he saw the crowds, he had compassion on them because they were confused and helpless, like sheep without a shepherd. He said to his disciples, "The harvest is great, but the workers are few. So pray to the Lord who is in charge of the harvest; ask him to send more workers into his fields."

SYNOPSIS

God has given you everything you need to successfully live a life of purpose and bring Him glory. The apostle Peter confirmed this truth when he said:

> **By his divine power, God has given us everything we need for living a godly life. We have received all of this by coming to know him, the one who called us to himself by means of his marvelous glory and excellence.**
>
> **— 2 Peter 1:3 (*NLT*)**

Friend, God has provided you with His amazing Word, the indwelling presence and power of the Holy Spirit, His divine anointing, and special spiritual gifts to accomplish all the good works He prepared and planned for you before you were born. The time for sitting and being a spectator in the bleachers is long gone. You are called by God to suit up and get into the game!

Jesus is our role model after whom we are to pattern our life. How did He see and do ministry? What can we learn from His life and apply to our own to maximize our level of effectiveness? That is what we will examine in this lesson.

The emphasis of this lesson:

Ministry requires all kinds of people doing all kinds of things — not just preaching and teaching God's Word and praying for people's healing. Although these things are extremely valuable and needed, people also need a pastoral touch. This indispensable form of relational ministry

is carried out not just by pastors, but also by caring people who have a pastoral heart.

Ministry Is Most Successful When All Christians Are Operating in Their Gifts

In Lesson 3, we saw how every believer has an important part to play in God's plans. Unfortunately, when many believers hear the word *ministry*, they automatically think, *That's for full-time pastors and church staff members*. But that is far from the truth. Ministry is something that all Christians do. Although it doesn't always look the same because each of us is equipped with different gifts, it is all rooted in the same heart of God and carried out in the same power of the Holy Spirit.

In Peter's first letter, he said, "God has given each of you a gift from his great variety of spiritual gifts. Use them well to serve one another" (1 Peter 4:10 *NLT*). He then asked, "Do you have the gift of speaking? Then speak as though God himself were speaking through you…" (1 Peter 4:11 *NLT*). *Speaking* would include preaching, teaching, prophesying, and exhorting. The fact is there are a myriad of different teachers and preachers. Some are fiery evangelists, and some are systematic teachers. Some are informational, and some are inspirational. The spectrum of this gift is wide, but regardless of the kind of speaking a person is gifted to do, he or she is to do it as though God Himself were speaking through them.

Peter then asked, "Do you have the gift of helping others? Do it with all the strength and energy that God supplies. Then everything you do will bring glory to God through Jesus Christ…" (1 Peter 4:11 *NLT*). Like speaking, the gift of helping is very diverse. Just think of all the gifted people who work behind the scenes to create Rick's TV program. The number of individuals needed to film, edit, produce, distribute, and air the show is much higher than you may think.

The same holds true for those who work in healthcare. If someone is needing surgery, most people will say, "The surgeon is most important." That may be true, but what about the nurses who prepare the room for the surgery and who sterilize all the tools and gather the right supplies? What about the technicians who dispense the correct anesthesia and the scrub techs and circulators who work directly with the patients to prepare them for surgery? And what about the post-op personnel who monitor the patient's progress and help him or her through rehabilitation?

The point is, every single person is important, and everyone's gift is equally valuable. Again, you will find that the greatest sense of fulfillment and excitement in your life will come as you are operating in your God-given gift.

What Do You Believe Is the Essence of Ministry?

Tony Cooke shared a passage of scripture that was very meaningful to him when he was a first-year Bible school student at Oral Roberts University (ORU) in 1979. Again and again, he heard messages taught from Matthew 9, where Matthew said:

> **Jesus traveled through all the towns and villages of that area, teaching in the synagogues and announcing the Good News about the Kingdom. And he healed every kind of disease and illness.**
>
> **— Matthew 9:35 (*NLT*)**

From the first time Tony heard this verse at age 20, he thought to himself, *That's what I want! I want to be just like Jesus — teaching, preaching, and healing.* In his mind, this was the apex and epitome of all ministry. Being behind the pulpit, teaching and preaching the Word publicly, and then periodically stepping away from the pulpit to lay hands on the sick who were standing in a prayer line was the end-all of ministry in his mind.

Ironically, when Tony was a Bible student at the university, he and his wife were selected to serve as the janitors of the church. Keep in mind, he wanted to go preach and save the world, so when he became the church janitor, he thought, *What's going on, God? You gave Billy Graham pulpits all over the world, but You've given my wife and me toilets all over the church. I don't get it.*

As it turned out, those years serving in maintenance were some of the best training for ministry Tony received. God taught him and his wife the value of serving, and that what goes on behind the pulpit is not the only important thing. The fact is, ministry requires all kinds of people to do all kinds of things — not just preaching, teaching, and praying for people's healing.

After being the janitor, Tony graduated to being an assistant pastor at that church where he was given many assignments such as inviting visitors to come back to church, distributing food through the church's food bank, and visiting and praying for people in the hospital. In his mind, these opportunities to help people were good, but they weren't nearly as exciting as speaking and praying for people in church.

At first, he didn't do much preaching and teaching. That didn't take place until the end of his three-and-a-half years of service. When he resigned to take a teaching position at Rhema Bible Training Center, he began to think about what he would share in his farewell sermon and what the people would come up and tell him after all his years of service at the church. *I've done all this teaching, preaching, and ministering in prayer lines,* he thought. *What are people going to come up and thank me for?*

Much to his surprise, after his final farewell sermon, people did come up and thank him, but their appreciation had nothing to do with any of the messages or series he taught. On the contrary, everything that people thanked him for were relational acts of service. For instance, people thanked him for coming to see them in the hospital; calling them when a loved one died; and for putting them in touch with someone who could help when they lost their job.

These actions proved true the words of Dr. Bennett, Rick's mentor who trained him for the ministry. Dr. Bennett said, "People will forget what you publicly preach, but they will never forget what you do for them." Although people usually can't remember what the pastor preached the previous week, they never forget the personal touch of things like flowers and phone calls in difficult times.

People Need a Pastoral Touch

Clearly, Tony was disappointed when no one came up and said thank you for a specific sermon or series he taught. Nevertheless, he decided to go back and reread the next verse of what he was taught in Bible school about Jesus' ministry. After Matthew talked about Jesus going around preaching, teaching, and healing people, he documented what Jesus did immediately afterward:

When he saw the crowds, he had compassion on them because they were confused and helpless, like sheep without a shepherd.
— Matthew 9:36 (*NLT*)

So after the teaching, preaching, and healing Jesus did in all the surrounding towns and villages, the people still had real-life needs that had to be met. That means…

- Although preaching is important, *people need more than sermons.*
- Although teaching is important, *people need more than lessons.*
- Although healing is important, *people need more than prayer lines.*

What people need is a *pastoral touch.* According to Jesus, the pastor is someone who stays with the flock and knows the sheep by name. The sheep know him, and he won't flee when a wolf comes. Moreover, a good pastor or shepherd is willing to go after the one sheep who has lost its way and has gone astray.

To be clear, teaching and preaching the Word of God and healing the sick are extremely valuable and necessary. But pastoral — or relational — ministry is equally important. This is the time when people are cared for and loved, which is what is designed to take place in the context of the local church.

Real love flowing through God's people builds bridges of relationships that connect people to Jesus and to each other.

After serving as the assistant pastor for three and a half years, Tony finally realized that ministry is more than messages and sermons. It is about more than what happens in the pulpit or a prayer line. What people remembered most about his years of serving were the relational things he did.

Anyone in the church can cook and bring people food. Likewise, you don't have to have a call to preach or graduate seminary to visit and pray for someone who is dying in the hospital. These are all relational touches that are pastoral in nature, and while a pastor can certainly carry out such tasks, anyone with a pastoral heart can minister in these ways. The pastoral touch expresses the heart of Jesus and leaves an impact that lasts a lifetime.

Three Levels of Ministry

To get a clearer picture of how Jesus saw ministry, let's take a moment and reread Matthew 9:35-38. The *New Living Translation* says it this way:

Jesus traveled through all the towns and villages of that area, teaching in the synagogues and announcing the Good News about the Kingdom. And he healed every kind of disease and illness. When he saw the crowds, he had compassion on them because they were confused and helpless, like sheep without a shepherd. He said to his disciples, "The harvest is great, but the workers are few. So pray to the Lord who is in charge of the harvest; ask him to send more workers into his fields."

From this passage, we can identify three levels of ministry taking place.

Level 1: Teaching, Preaching, Healing

The foundational level of ministry is what the Bible classifies as the five-fold ministry gifts. This makes up a very small minority of individuals who are called into the Body of Christ to preach, teach, and bring healing to people. This group is made up of "…the apostles, the prophets, the evangelists, and the pastors and teachers" (Ephesians 4:11 *NLT*).

Those who are part of a "spectator church" mistakenly believe that the pastor or preacher is the one who does all the work. But that is not the case. Yes, a pastor is called by God to minister to people and preach and teach the Word. However, his ultimate purpose is to equip the people in the congregation to do the work of the ministry.

Level 2: Pastoral Care

The second level of ministry can be done by the pastor, but it is also to be carried out by both church staff and volunteers who have a pastoral heart and serve as an extension of the pastor as well as an extension of Jesus, the Great Shepherd Himself. These individuals operate in the gift of mercy and kindness, which we saw described in Romans 12:8. (Note: In the New Testament, the words *shepherd* and *pastor* are translated from the same Greek word. Thus, they carry the same meaning.)

Level 3: "Workers in the Field"

The third level of ministry has the largest number of people, and Jesus refers to them as "workers in the field." In Matthew 9:37 and 38 (*NLT*), He said, "The harvest is great, but the *workers* are few. So pray to the Lord who is in charge of the harvest; ask him to send more *workers into his fields*."

There's great work to be done, but there are not many workers. This is where the bulk of the Body of Christ comes into play. Very few believers are called to the fivefold ministry of apostles, prophets, evangelists, pastors, and teachers (level 1). However, *everyone* can be a worker and contribute to meeting the needs of those who are "ripe for harvest."

Think about all the people who serve in the local church. Greeters and ushers are the "first face" of the church, gifted by God to exude kindness and love to everyone. Technicians, custodians, and worship and choir team members all usually show up at church hours before the pastor. And don't forget the prayer warriors. All these individuals have to deal with their own flesh and work through personal problems at home before they arrive at church. They are gifted by God and instrumental to preparing the surroundings and the people to experience God's presence before the pastor steps into the pulpit to deliver the Word.

A Real-Life Example of a 'Worker in the Field'

Tony shared a story of a pastor who was looking for a church many years ago. When he and his wife arrived at a certain church, they met a greeter who wasn't on duty and was standing under an awning near the entrance. With a baby in one arm, a cast on her leg, and a crutch cradling her shoulder, she saw this man and his wife drive in not knowing where to go. Immediately, she hobbled out with her baby, nursery bag, and crutch and said, "Can I help you?"

After showing them where to park, she walked them into the building, showed them where to take their children, and introduced them to the teachers. She then led them to the sanctuary and connected them with some regular attendees who were about their age and who helped them find a seat.

In that moment, *before* the church service had even started, this man's wife turned to him and said, "This is where we're going to go to church."

The man responded, "Are you sure? You haven't even heard the worship or the sermon yet."

"I'm sure," she said. "I don't have to hear the music, the worship, or the sermon. If the people are loving, caring, and serving like this woman who met us in the parking lot, this is the kind of church I want to attend."

Amazingly, this off-duty greeter with a gift of hospitality was the game-changer for this visiting couple. Her sacrificial service as a doorkeeper in the house of God was the personal, pastoral touch this pastor's wife needed to confirm what church she and her family were to attend.

It's important for us to see this full scope of ministry and not just have a distorted, narrow perspective that thinks all valuable ministry happens behind the pulpit. Indeed, the life-giving power of a pastoral touch expresses the heart of Jesus and leaves an impact that lasts a lifetime.

QUESTIONS AND ANSWERS WITH RICK RENNER

In the program, Rick answered the following question from one of our viewers.

Q. How do I hear God and know His will for my life?

A. That's an important question because your success in life depends on you knowing the will of God for your life and obediently walking it out.

God will speak to you very clearly through His Word and reveal His general will for your life. He will also speak to you by His Spirit, through your pastor as he or she teaches, through various voices of authority in your life, and through other people in the Body of Christ.

He may even speak to you through circumstances and situations to direct your steps. The fact is that there are a variety of ways God speaks to you and directs you, and when all of these things begin to line up, it's like Him giving you a "green light" to go forward in a specific direction.

If you would like to learn how to know the voice of God and know His will for your life, we recommend Rick's series called *How to Know the Will of God*, which is one of the best series he has ever taught. You can order it online at **renner.org** or by calling 1-800-742-5593.

A Prayer To Receive Salvation

If you've never received Jesus as your Savior and Lord, there's no better time for you to experience the new life Jesus wants to give you. To receive God's gift of salvation through Jesus, pray this prayer from your heart:

Jesus, I repent of my sin and receive You as my Savior and Lord. Wash away my sin with Your precious Blood and make me completely new.

*I thank You that my sin is removed, and Satan no longer has any
right to lay claim on me. Through Your empowering grace, I faithfully
promise that I will serve You as my Lord for the rest of my life. In Your
name, amen.*

If you just prayed this prayer of salvation, you are born again! You are
a brand-new creation in Christ! Would you please let us know of your
decision by going to **renner.org/salvation**? We would love to connect
with you and pray for you as you begin your new life in Christ.

STUDY QUESTIONS

**Study to shew thyself approved unto God, a workman that
needeth not to be ashamed, rightly dividing the word of truth.**
— 2 Timothy 2:15

1. According to Ephesians 4:10-16, what are the fivefold ministry gifts,
    who gave them to the Church, and what is their purpose? (To help
    you achieve this purpose, also consider what the apostle Paul also said
    in Acts 20:32; 1 Corinthians 13:11 and 14:20.)

2. *Pastors* are one of the fivefold ministry gifts in the Church. According to
    Scripture, what are their primary responsibilities to God's people? Read
    the following verses for three specific things pastors are called to do:

    • Jeremiah 3:15 and 23:4; Ezekiel 34:23; 1 Peter 5:2; Matthew 20:26

    • Isaiah 62:6; Ezekiel 3:17; Hebrews 13:7

    • Matthew 28:19,20; 1 Timothy 3:1,2 and 4:11; 2 Corinthians 4:1,2

PRACTICAL APPLICATION

**But be ye doers of the word, and not hearers only,
deceiving your own selves.**
—James 1:22

1. In Tony Cooke's mind, at one time in his life the apex and epitome of
    all ministry was teaching, preaching, and healing. As you began this
    lesson, what was your understanding of the main emphasis of minis-
    try? How has this teaching reshaped your understanding?

2. Without question, we all need the teaching and preaching of God's
    Word, along with His healing power. But what we also desperately

need is a genuine *pastoral touch*. In what specific ways have you personally experienced this relational, pastoral expression of ministry? Who has God used in your life to be an extension of Jesus in this way? How have their caring actions impacted and influenced your life?

TOPIC

Multi-Dimensional Ministry

SCRIPTURES

Ephesians 3:17-19 (*NLT*) — Then Christ will make his home in your hearts as you trust in him. Your roots will grow down into God's love and keep you strong. And may you have the power to understand, as all God's people should, how wide, how long, how high, and how deep his love is. May you experience the love of Christ, though it is too great to understand fully. Then you will be made complete with all the fullness of life and power that comes from God.

SYNOPSIS

In Lesson 4, we learned that in addition to teaching, preaching, and healing, which are extremely valuable and needed, people also need a pastoral touch. This vital form of relational ministry is carried out by pastors as well as caring believers who are gifted by God with a pastoral heart. Erlita Renner, Rick's mom, is a perfect example of someone who operated in this way.

Indeed, not all ministry happens from the pulpit. A great deal of ministry takes place one-on-one through pastoral care. Jesus exemplified this type of relational interaction everywhere He went. As you read through the gospels, you will see that in every town and village, He was reaching out and touching people all the time — the woman at the well, the paralytic, the blind, the lame, the lepers, and on and on the list goes.

We saw in our last lesson that after Jesus taught, preached, and healed, He was moved with compassion because the people were like sheep without a shepherd (*see* Matthew 9:35,36). They were still in need of love, care, and attention, which is what everyone needs. Sermons and Christian resources are great, but sometimes people just need someone to look them in the eye and say, "I believe in you! You're going to make it! Everything is going to be okay." It's this personal touch that carries tremendous weight and is something every believer — including you — has the capacity to do!

The emphasis of this lesson:

The love of God is multi-dimensional, reaching out in all directions. God's love meets us right where we are; His love goes the distance to reach all who are far from Him; His love sends us soaring with praise and worship; and His love matures us, anchoring us deeply in solid, biblical teaching. We all need deep roots in God's love to keep us strong.

You Have What It Takes To Be a Blessing!

So many people in this world today are lonely and untouched. If you listen for the voice of the Holy Spirit, He will give you ample opportunities to use your hands to release His power through your touch. Your hands are powerful, and they can infuse others with strength, hope, and encouragement.

Years ago, it was a common practice of many pastors to stand at the back door of the church every week and shake hands with each person as they left. In some cases, these pastors would stand and personally touch hundreds, sometimes thousands, of people and offer them an encouraging word.

It is safe to say that after pouring out their heart through preaching and teaching the Word, they were tired and wanted to go home and get something to eat just like everyone else. Nevertheless, they chose to make that personal, pastoral connection with each person. It was a great sacrifice, but it produced a great impact — and it is still impacting people today.

At the Moscow Good News Church, for example, attendees look forward to the end of each service every week when they can make that personal connection with the pastor. What is amazing is that you don't have to be a pastor or even serve on staff at your church to be used by God in this way.

If you're a born-again believer, the Spirit of God lives in you, and you have His anointing (*see* 1 John 2:20,27). Your touch can release healing, and your words can impart blessing to anyone with whom you come in contact. We were made for community, and people need what you have to give them.

We All Need Deep Roots in the Love of God

One of the most important aspects of God's character that we need to understand is His *love*. When the apostle Paul wrote to the believers in Ephesus, he described the multi-dimensional love of God. Specifically, in Ephesians 3:17-19 (*NLT*), he said:

> **Then Christ will make his home in your hearts as you trust in him. Your roots will grow down into God's love and keep you strong. And may you have the power to understand, as all God's people should, how wide, how long, how high, and how deep his love is. May you experience the love of Christ, though it is too great to understand fully. Then you will be made complete with all the fullness of life and power that comes from God.**

Please realize that this passage — like most of the New Testament letters — was written to entire churches. So, while we can — and should — read the Bible to understand how it personally applies to us, we must also read it to understand how it applies to all of us *corporately* as the Church.

What all of us need is in these verses. When we trust in Christ, He will make His home in our hearts. Likewise, as we trust in Him, our roots will grow down into God's love and keep us strong, and that is what we all need — deep roots in the love of God (*see* Ephesians 3:17).

The cry of Paul's heart — which is really the cry of God's heart — is that all of God's people would have the power to understand "…how wide, how long, how high, and how deep his love is" (Ephesians 3:18 *NLT*).

And God doesn't want us to just know *about* His love — He wants us to personally experience His love and be made complete with all the fullness of His life and power living inside us.

The Love of God Is
Wide, Long, High, and Deep

What Does It Mean That God's Love Is 'Wide'?

Reflecting on a time of ministry overseas, Tony stated that unlike many people living in the United States who are "super-sized" in stature, most who live in the Far East are of a much smaller frame. Consequently, things are made smaller to accommodate the size of the people. On one occasion many years ago, just before ministering at a church in the Far East, Tony became wedged in his seat because it was so narrow. In fact, the chair was so confining he felt as if he was sitting in a vice grip.

Turning to his wife, Lisa, Tony urgently whispered, "Honey, I'm stuck! I don't know if I'm going to be able to get out of this chair."

With his circulation quickly being cut off from his legs and just moments to spare, Tony pleaded, "When the pastor introduces me to speak, I'm going to thrust myself forward. PLEASE put your hand on my back and push me as hard as you can!"

Thankfully, Tony's plan worked, and Lisa was able to bring deliverance to her chair-bound husband that day.

After being cast out of that narrow seat, he began thinking of how uncomfortable, restricting, and unwelcoming it felt. *Whoever designed these chairs*, he said to himself, *didn't have someone of my size in mind.*

Similarly, when the Bible talks about the love of God being *wide*, it means His love is unrestricted, welcoming, and comfortable. It's like a loved one you haven't seen for a long time standing with his arms outstretched wide, communicating love and acceptance.

That's the picture of the "wide" love of God. In His love, He meets all of us right where we are.

When Jesus met the woman at the well, He talked to her about living water. When He met the Jewish leader, Nicodemus, He talked to him using theological concepts he was familiar with and could understand. Moreover, when Jesus spoke with Peter, James, and John, He used fishermen's terms they could easily grasp. Amazingly, Jesus could speak everyone's language and meet them right at their level.

So, when you think of the *width* of God's love, think of connecting with people right where they are.

What Does It Mean That God's Love Is 'Long'?

When we think of *length*, we often think of distance — something that is far away. This should cause us to think of not just reaching people in far distant lands, but also those who may be close to us geographically but far away from God.

So while the width of God's love equates to accepting people who are coming to Him, the length of God's love equates to going after people who are *not* coming to Him. Thus, God is going the distance to reach people far from Him, which is what we often do through missions, evangelism, and various outreaches.

What Does It Mean That God's Love Is 'High'?

When we think of *height*, we think of something soaring high into the sky. Hence, the height of God's love is all about raising the roof with thanksgiving, worship, and praise. The Bible says, "Let the high praises of God be in their mouth, and a two-edged sword in their hand" (Psalm 149:6).

The calling and gifting of worship leaders is to help people rise above the lowly circumstances and difficult situations in which they find themselves and enter the presence of God. Psalm 100:4 tells us that we enter the gates of God's presence by giving Him thanks, and if we want to draw even closer, we can enter His inner courts by giving Him praise. Worship elevates us into the Holy of Holies.

What Does It Mean That God's Love Is 'Deep?

When we think of *depth*, we often think of something that goes deep into the ground — something that is deeply grounded and immovable. When a skyscraper is constructed, engineers and excavators must go deep into the ground to lay a foundation that is strong enough and solid enough to sustain the structure that will reach into the sky.

Thus, the depth of God's love is all about taking people into spiritual maturity. This would include strong biblical teaching, in-depth study, and discipleship.

Putting it all together...

- The **width** of God's love relates to His *hospitality, acceptance,* and *fellowship.*
- The **length** of God's love relates to *evangelism, missions,* and *outreach.*
- The **height** of God's love relates to the *worship and praise of God.*
- The **depth** of God's love relates to being *grounded in the mature meat of the Word.*

A Balance of Effort in All Areas Is Required

It is interesting to note that in nearly every church, there seems to be a specific bent toward one of these four categories. For instance, some churches major on the width of God's love, saying, "Missions and evangelism are most important, so we should be more evangelistic." In other churches, the length of God's love is the consensus, positioning fellowship and acceptance as the principal thing. At the same time, there are also churches that lean strongly in the direction of height, making praise and worship the supreme priority. Then there are other churches where the depth of God's love is the emphasis, and they designate the study of the Word as paramount to everything else.

The truth is, we need to have a balance of emphasis in all four of these areas. Although it is not wrong for individuals and churches to have a preference, we need a blend of all four facets of God's love. And God has gifted His people to function in all these areas.

Friend, avoid the tendency to put other people down because they have a different propensity than you. Instead, ask God to help you learn to appreciate what everyone else can contribute.

This is the end of the age, and God needs all of us to answer the call to full engagement in service to Him. We've got to get out of the grandstands and get out onto the playing field. God has given us the knowledge of His truth, the power of His Spirit, and the gifts of His grace so that we have everything we need to play the game of faith all the way to victory.

Father, help us to accept Your call to get out of the bleachers and get onto the field and play with gusto all the way to victory. In Jesus' Name, Amen!

QUESTIONS AND ANSWERS WITH RICK RENNER

In the program, Rick answered the following question from one of our viewers.

Q. What if I'm giving my tithes and offerings but I see no financial increase in my life?

A. We're told in Galatians 6:7, "Be not deceived; God is not mocked: for whatsoever a man soweth, that shall he also reap." Here we find that sowing and reaping is a divine law that is never violated and never mocked. What you sow, you will reap.

If you sow a seed today, it may take time before you begin to reap your harvest. Just as a farmer puts his seed into the ground and doesn't expect to come back to the field the next day and find a big harvest, you, too, must not expect overnight results from your giving.

There is a period of waiting before the harvest comes. But that doesn't mean you abandon your seed. Instead, you keep watering it with the Word (speaking God's promises aloud), and you continue to faithfully sow your seed, giving your tithes and your offerings. Remember, if we don't grow weary in well doing, "…in due season we shall reap, if we faint not" (Galatians 6:9).

A Prayer To Receive Salvation

If you've never received Jesus as your Savior and Lord, there's no better time for you to experience the new life Jesus wants to give you. To receive God's gift of salvation through Jesus, pray this prayer from your heart:

> *Jesus, I repent of my sin and receive You as my Savior and Lord. Wash away my sin with Your precious Blood and make me completely new. I thank You that my sin is removed, and Satan no longer has any right to lay claim on me. Through Your empowering grace, I faithfully promise that I will serve You as my Lord for the rest of my life. In Your name, Amen.*

If you just prayed this prayer of salvation, you are born again! You are a brand-new creation in Christ! Would you please let us know of your decision by going to **renner.org/salvation**? We would love to connect with you and pray for you as you begin your new life in Christ.

STUDY QUESTIONS

> Study to shew thyself approved unto God, a workman that
> needeth not to be ashamed, rightly dividing the word of truth.
> — 2 Timothy 2:15

1. Love is not just something God does — *love is who God is!*
   (*See* 1 John 4:8, 16.) What do you know about the love of God?
   Consider these fundamental declarations from Scripture:

   • How does God demonstrate His love? (*See* John 3:16; 15:13;
   Romans 5:8; 1 John 4:9,10.)

   • How great is the power of God's love? (*See* Romans 8:35-39.)

   • How do you receive God's love, and how does His love grow in
   you? (*See* Romans 5:5; 1 John 4:11-12,16-17.)

2. Having a *heart revelation* of God's love is indescribably powerful!
   According to First John 4:18 (*AMPC*), what is one of the most
   empowering effects of understanding God's love?

   **There is no fear in love [dread does not exist], but full-
   grown (complete, perfect) love turns fear out of doors
   and expels every trace of terror! For fear brings with it the
   thought of punishment, and [so] he who is afraid has not
   reached the full maturity of love [is not yet grown into
   love's complete perfection].**

   Pray and ask the Holy Spirit to give you a continually unfolding
   revelation of God's love for you.

PRACTICAL APPLICATION

> But be ye doers of the word, and not hearers only,
> deceiving your own selves.
> — James 1:22

It is God's deepest desire, "[That you may really come] to know [prac-
tically, through experience for yourselves] the love of Christ, which far
surpasses mere knowledge [without experience]; that you may be filled
[through all your being] unto all the fullness of God [may have the richest
measure of the divine Presence, and become a body wholly filled and
flooded with God Himself]!" (Ephesians 3:19 *AMPC*).

1. In what ways have you personally experienced for yourself the tangible love of God? Briefly describe one or two situations where He demonstrated His love and explain how it affected you.

2. Why is personal experience of God's love far greater and more meaningful than mere knowledge without experience?

3. If you have not tasted of God's love — or you have children, grandchildren, or loved ones who are unaware of His love — begin to pray:

   Heavenly Father, I ask You to make Your love for me — and for my children, grandchildren, and loved ones [speak their names] — real. Begin to give us personal experiences in our lives that tangibly demonstrate Your immeasurable love. And as You do, fill us with the fullness of Your love — may we have the richest measure of Your divine presence and become totally filled and flooded with You. Thank You, Father. In Jesus' name, amen!

NOTES

[1] Cooke, Tony. *The End of Spectator Church: Answering God's Call to Full Engagement.* Shippensburg, PA: Harrison House Publishers, 2023.

Notes

Notes

Notes

CLAIM YOUR FREE RESOURCE!

As a way of introducing you further to the teaching ministry of Rick Renner, we would like to send you FREE of charge his teaching, "How To Receive a Miraculous Touch From God" on CD or as an MP3 download.

In His earthly ministry, Jesus commonly healed *all* who were sick of *all* their diseases. In this profound message, learn about the manifold dimensions of Christ's wisdom, goodness, power, and love toward all humanity who came to Him in faith with their needs.

☑ **YES, I want to receive Rick Renner's monthly teaching letter!**

Simply scan the QR code to claim this resource or go to:
renner.org/claim-your-free-offer

WITH US!